The Mighty T. Rex

Brianna Kaiser

BUMBA BOOKS™

LERNER PUBLICATIONS ◆ MINNEAPOLIS

Note to Educators

Throughout this book, you'll find critical-thinking questions. These can be used to engage young readers in thinking critically about the topic and in using the text and photos to do so.

Lerner Publications Company
An imprint of Lerner Publishing Group, Inc.
241 First Avenue North
Minneapolis, MN 55401 USA

For reading levels and more information, look up this title at www.lernerbooks.com.

Main body text set in Helvetica Textbook Com Roman.
Typeface provided by Linotype AG.

Library of Congress Cataloging-in-Publication Data

Names: Kaiser, Brianna, 1996– author.
Title: The mighty T. rex / Brianna Kaiser.
Description: Minneapolis : Lerner Publications , [2022] | Series: Bumba books - mighty dinosaurs | Audience: Ages 4–7 | Audience: Grades K–1 | Summary: "T. rex was about as long as a school bus and weighed about as much as an elephant! Meet these giant beasts and discover their traits and habitats"— Provided by publisher.
Identifiers: LCCN 2021005553 | ISBN 9781728441023 (library binding) | ISBN 9781728444499 (ebook)
Subjects: LCSH: Tyrannosaurus rex—Juvenile literature.
Classification: LCC QE862.S3 K34 2022 | DDC 567.912/9—dc23

LC record available at https://lccn.loc.gov/2021005553

Manufactured in the United States of America
1-49872-49717-5/6/2021

Table of
Contents

King of the Dinosaurs

Tyrannosaurus rex, or T. rex, was a type of dinosaur. It lived sixty-six to sixty-eight million years ago. Dinosaurs are extinct.

T. rex lived in forests and river valleys in western North America.

Why do you think T. rex lived in forests and river valleys?

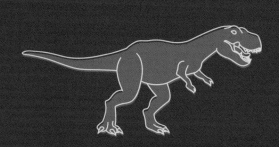

T. rex was large. It was
about as long and tall as
a school bus!

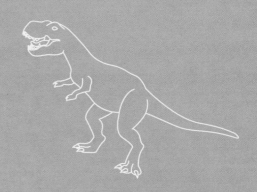

It was heavy. Each one
weighed about as much
as an elephant.

T. rex had small arms.

Each arm had two

fingers with claws.

T. rex moved on two legs.

What other animals move on two legs?

It had a strong sense of smell. This helped it find prey. T. rex ate meat.

It had a powerful jaw and about sixty pointed teeth. Each tooth was about 8 inches (20 cm) long.

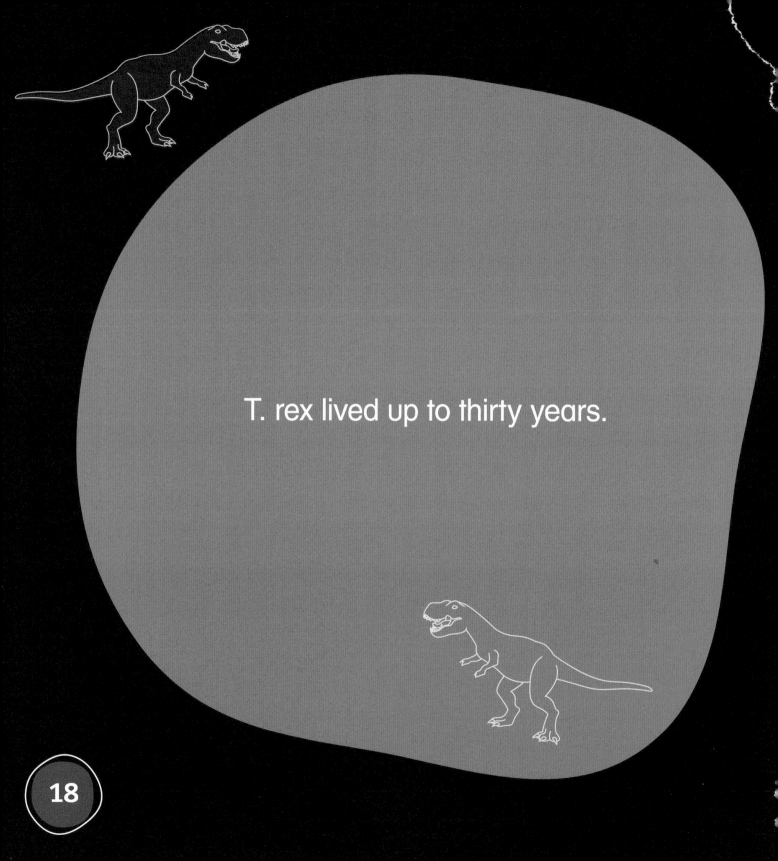

T. rex lived up to thirty years.

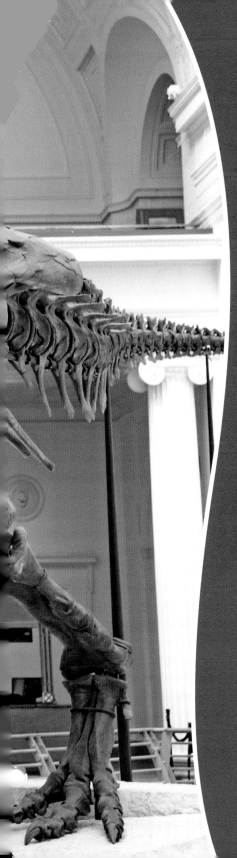

Today, scientists learn more about T. rex by studying fossils.

Parts of a T. Rex

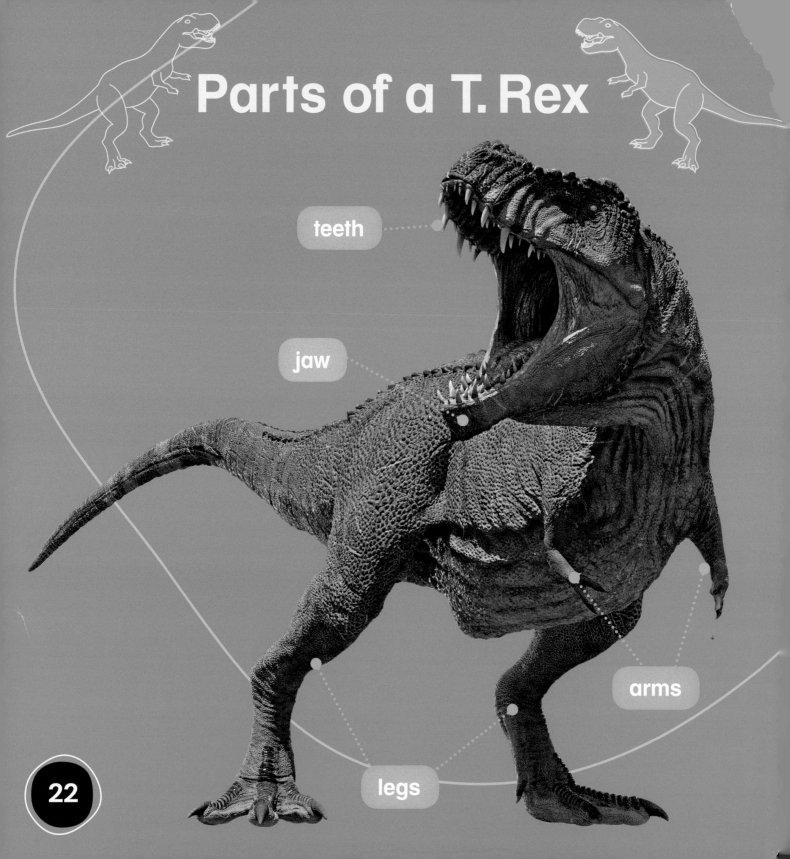

teeth

jaw

arms

legs

Picture Glossary

extinct

no longer alive

fossil

a trace of a living animal from a long time ago

prey

an animal that is hunted by another animal

river valley

a low area of land with a river running through it

Learn More

Kaiser, Brianna. *The Mighty Brontosaurus.* Minneapolis: Lerner Publications, 2022.

Murray, Julie. *Tyrannosaurus Rex.* Minneapolis: Abdo Zoom, 2020.

York, M. J. *Dinosaurs.* Mankato, MN: Child's World, 2021.

Index

Photo Credits